NATURAL WONDERS

K2

The Savage Mountain

Christine Webster

WEIGL PUBLISHERS INC.

Published by Weigl Publishers Inc.
350 5th Avenue, Suite 3304, PMB 6G
New York, NY 10118-0069

Website: www.weigl.com

Library of Congress Cataloging-in-Publication Data

Webster, Christine.
  K2: natural wonders/Christine Webster.
        p. cm.
  ISBN: 978-1-59036-939-5 (soft cover: alk. Paper) –
  ISBN: 978-1-59036-938-8 (hard cover: alk. Paper)
  1. K2 (Pakistan: Mountain)—Juvenile literature. I. Title.
GB546.K13W43 2009
551.43'20954913—dc22

2008015663

Printed in the United States of America

1 2 3 4 5 6 7 8 9 0   12 11 10 09 08

Project Coordinators
Heather Kissock
and Heather C. Hudak

Design
Terry Paulhus

Photograph Credits

Weigl acknowledges Getty Images as its primary image supplier.

Every reasonable effort has been made to trace ownership and to obtain permission to reprint copyright material. The publishers would be pleased to have any errors or omissions brought to their attention so that they may be corrected in subsequent printings.

Contents

The Savage Mountain

K2 is the second-highest mountain in the world, after Mount Everest. Located in Asia's Karakoram Mountain Range, K2 is referred to as Ketu. This is the name given to the mountain by the area's Balti people.

Although Mount Everest is taller, K2 is a more challenging climb. About 2,600 people have climbed Mount Everest and succeeded. Yet, only 280 people have completed the climb up K2.

K2 is hard to climb for many reasons. The extreme **altitude** makes oxygen sparse. The mountain also experiences major storms that can last for days. Despite these conditions, many people think this savage mountain is the ultimate climb.

K2 is also referred to as Mount Godwin-Austen in honor of the first man to survey the mountain.

K2 Facts

- K2 reaches 28,251 feet (8,611 meters) and is the highest mountain in Pakistan.

- K2 has a collection of dark brown and black **metamorphic** rocks. Karakoram means "black gravel" or "black mountain."

- Besides Ketu and Mount Godwin-Austen, the mountain is called Chogo Ri. This means "Big Mountain."

- K2's incline is the steepest of any mountain in the world. Its peak is pyramid-shaped, meaning it drops dramatically on every side.

- The "K" in K2 stands for Karakoram. The "2" indicates that it was the second mountain to be noted by surveyors. The "2" is now said to represent the mountain's second-highest standing.

The K2 Locator

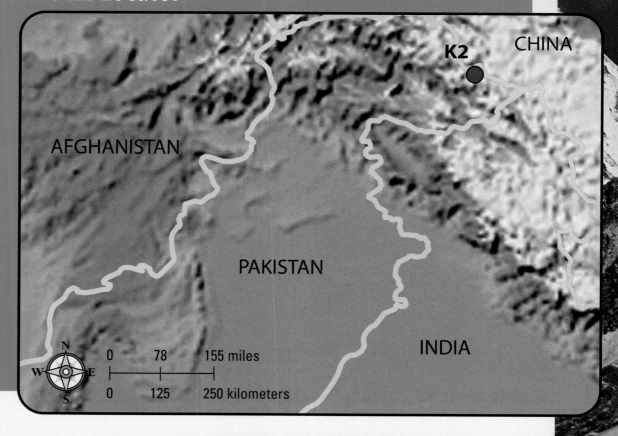

AFGHANISTAN

CHINA

K2

PAKISTAN

INDIA

N
W · E
S

| 0 | 78 | 155 miles |
| 0 | 125 | 250 kilometers |

Where in the World?

The Karakoram Mountain Range is located in northeast Pakistan and northern India near the Chinese border. The range extends 300 miles (480 km) southeast and runs between the Indus and Yarkant Rivers. This region has some of the highest mountains on Earth. It also has many of the world's longest **glaciers**. K2 rises from the Godwin-Austen glacier.

K2 is found on the border between Pakistan and China. India's Kashmir province is to its southeast. The mountain lies in a remote area. It is more than 65 miles (105 km) from any village.

Climbers cross the Godwin-Austen Glacier to reach K2.

Puzzler

Q The Karakoram Mountain Range is just one of many mountain ranges in the world. Ranges can be found on every continent. Each has its own highest mountain. Using your local library or the Internet, research mountain ranges around the world. Then, match the mountains with the correct mountain ranges from the lists below.

1. The Rockies
2. The Andes
3. The Alps
4. The Caucasus
5. The Himalayas

A. Mont Blanc
B. Mount Elbert
C. Mount Aconcagua
D. Mount Everest
E. Mount Elbrus

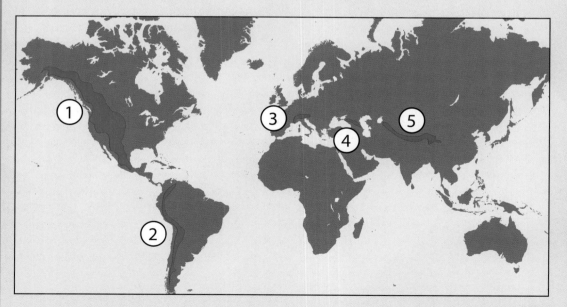

 1) B 2) C 3) A 4) E 5) D

A Trip Back in Time

The Karakoram Mountain Range began to take shape millions of years ago. At this time, activity that took place deep underground caused part of the Earth's **crust** to surge upward.

Over time, the mountain range was shaped by a series of **ice ages**. During these years, glaciers covered the area. As these huge sheets of ice shifted, they deposited and removed **sediment**, creating valleys and jagged peaks. This led to the rugged terrain that makes up K2.

After the ice ages, **erosion** began to mold the shape of the mountain. High winds weathered, or broke down, the exposed rock.

The Karakorams continue to face erosion today.

How a Mountain Forms

Earth's crust is made up of several pieces called tectonic plates. The plates float on a layer of melted rock called magma. Sometimes, the magma pushes the plates into each other. The force of the collision pushes the plates upward. This is how mountains form.

The Karakoram Mountain Range formed as a result of a collision between two plates. At one time, the country of India was not connected to a continent. The movement of tectonic plates pushed it toward the Asian continent. When the plate on which India sits collided with the plate that holds Asia, the force caused parts of the plates to break off and move upward. This formed the Karakoram Mountain Range and many other nearby mountain ranges, including the Himalayas.

■ Today, India is still moving north about 2 inches (5 centimeters) per year. As a result, each year, the Karakorams gain about 0.25 inches (7 millimeters) in height.

Plants in the K2 Ecosystem

Like any mountain, K2 has many **ecosystems**. **Elevation** plays a major role in the types of plants and animals found on the mountain and the part of the mountain on which they live. As a mountain gains altitude, the air becomes colder and thinner. This limits the types of plants that can live at higher elevations.

At the lower levels of K2, there is a good supply of oxygen and melting glaciers that supply water. As a result, the area is home to many types of plants. **Deciduous** trees, such as elm and poplar trees, are found up to 7,000 feet (2,134 m) from the mountain base. At that point, the forests become **coniferous**. Fir, pine, and spruce trees are scattered throughout. Juniper is found on high slopes.

As the air gets thinner and there are fewer water sources, plants become smaller in size. Trees are replaced by shrubs and small alpine flowers. At the snow line, or the part of the mountain that is covered with snow year-round, plant life no longer grows.

■ **Wildflowers are a common sight on K2.**

Curious Climate

No one has ever climbed K2 in the winter—for good reason. Winters on the K2 are harsh and cold. Heavy snowfall, strong winds, and raging storms that last for days are common. At the higher levels of the mountain, temperatures remain lower than 32 degrees Fahrenheit (0 degrees Celsius) year-round.

In May and June, spring arrives on the lower levels of K2. This season is known for its stable weather and high temperatures. In these months, some of K2's snow will melt, and the snow line will start higher up the mountain.

In July and August, the weather changes again. The lower elevations have heavy rains brought on by **monsoons**. These seasonal storms come from the Indian Ocean, to the south of the Karakoram range.

■ **The best climbing season is from May until September.**

Animal Life on K2

As is the case of plant life, the types of animal found on K2 depend on the elevation of the mountain. Animal life is far more abundant on the foothills and lower slopes. It is here that animals such as the Asiatic black bear and clouded leopard reside.

Many types of mountain goats live farther up the mountain, in areas that are less forested and more rocky. The Siberian ibex and markbor are two types of goats found on the craggy slopes of K2. The area is also home to Marco Polo sheep. Other animals living above the tree line include the snow leopard, red panda, and Tibetan yak.

Birds can often be seen flying at K2's higher elevations. The Himalayan griffon, a member of the vulture family, and the golden eagle are two of the more common sights.

▬ **The golden eagle can fly at speeds up to 80 miles (129 km) per hour.**

Mountain Mammal

The Siberian ibex is one of the few animals that can survive the harsh climate and rugged terrain of K2. The ibex stands at about 3 feet (0.9 m) in height and can weigh up to 285 pounds (130 kilograms). Often, these goats are light tan in color, but males can be much darker. Both males and females have beards, with the female's beard being smaller than that of the male.

Like many mountain goats, the Siberian ibex has horns. A male's horns grow into huge arcs that curl over his back. A female's horns bend only slightly toward the rear.

The Siberian ibex can be found at about 16,000 feet (6,000 m), but it will head to lower parts of the mountain when winter arrives. The lower slopes are fairly steep, making it difficult for snow piles to form. This means that food is easier to find. If snow cover is heavy, the Siberian ibex uses its sharp hooves to paw through the snow to the plants underneath.

■ **The life span of the Siberian ibex is six years.**

Early Explorers

K2 was first surveyed in 1856 by a group of Europeans. The team was led by Thomas Mongomerie, a lieutenant with Great Britain's Royal Engineers. He studied the **topography** of the mountain from an observation post at the top of Haramukh Peak in Kashmir, more than 137 miles (220 km) away. Mongomerie named 32 summits in the Karakoram Range. K2 was the second peak that he saw.

In 1861, Henry Haversham Godwin-Austen went into the Karakorams to do a more detailed survey of the area. He was the first person to accurately describe and map the terrain of the K2.

For many years, people believed K2 was impossible to climb. After Godwin-Austen completed his survey, people began to think about climbing the mountain. In 1902, Europeans Oscar Eckenstein and Aleister Crowley were the first people to try to climb K2. They were unsuccessful. Many more attempts were made over the next 40 years, and in 1954, Italians Lino Lacedelli and Achille Compagnoni reached the summit.

Still, the mountain continues to be a challenge for climbers. Fewer than 300 people have completed the climb. More that 60 others have died trying.

In 2004, celebrations were held in honor of the 50th anniversary of the first successful climb up K2.

Biography

Henry Haversham Godwin-Austin

Henry Haversham Godwin-Austen was a British soldier, surveyor, topographer, and geologist. In 1851, he entered the army in Sandhurst, England. Godwin-Austen climbed the ranks to lieutenant-colonel. Much of his career was spent in India. He fought in the Punjab and Burmese wars. In 1856, Godwin-Austen joined the Trigonometrical Survey of India. For 21 years, he surveyed the land around K2 and the mountain itself. The mountain and a glacier were named in honor of his efforts.

Godwin-Austen was a published writer. His books were mainly about nature. His best-known book is called *The Land and Freshwater Mollusca of India (1882-1887)*. Another book, *Birds of Assam (1870–78)*, contains the first written descriptions of many of the birds found in India.

Facts of Life

Born: July 6, 1834

Hometown: Teignmouth, England

Occupation: British soldier, surveyor, topographer, and geologist

Died: December 2, 1932

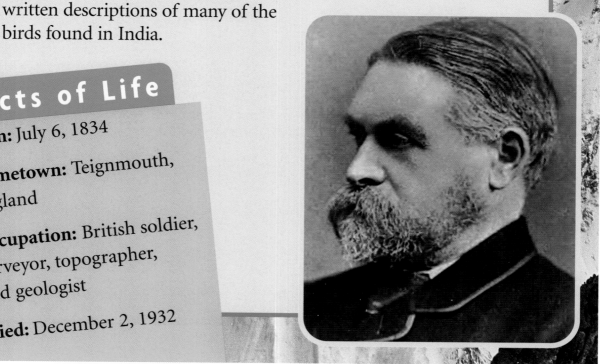

The Big Picture

The world's ten highest mountains are all located in southern Asia. With the exception of K2, all of these mountains are found in the Himalayas Range.

2

9

PAKISTAN

INDIA

N
W   E
S

| 0 | 78 | 155 miles |

| 0 | 125 | 250 kilometers |

Map Legend

	Mountain	Location	Height (m)	Height (ft)
1.	Mount Everest	Nepal	8,850	29,035
2.	K2	Pakistan	8,611	28,250
3.	Kangchenjunga	Nepal	8,586	28,169
4.	Lhotse	Nepal	8,501	27,920
5.	Makalu I	Nepal	8,462	27,765
6.	Cho Oyu	Nepal	8,201	26,906
7.	Dhaulagiri	Nepal	8,167	26,794
8.	Manaslu I	Nepal	8,156	26,758
9.	Nanga Parbat	Pakistan	8,125	26,658
10.	Annapurna I	Nepal	8,091	26,545

CHINA

NEPAL

Living on K2

Although remote, the land around K2 is home to different cultural groups. These include the Shina, the Gujar, the Wakhi, and the Balti. Often, these groups live in the traditional ways of their ancestors. They have little contact with the other parts of the world.

Despite its harsh environment, K2 provides the basic needs for the people who live around it. They grow crops on valley floors and on terraces that are carved into valley sides. Main crops include wheat, barley, apricots, walnuts, and vegetables.

Land for animal farming is important on K2. The dry, rocky lower slopes have small grazing areas. Larger pastures are found on the higher peaks. Farm animals include goats, sheep, and chickens.

Rain is not a constant in the Karakorams. Life on K2 relies on water from melting glaciers. Glacier water is distributed by a system of canals. Sometimes, these human-made canals cross the sides of cliffs that stretch several feet high.

■ **The Balti are just one of the cultural groups that live near Skardu, a town near the K2 base camp.**

Conserving K2

The Mountain Areas **Conservancy** Project (MACP) was formed in 2006 to help protect plants and animals in the Karakoram, Hindukush, and Western Himalayan Mountain Ranges. Through the project, communities learn how they can help care for the environment.

MACP works with many organizations, such as the World Wildlife Foundation Pakistan, the Aga Khan Rural Support Program, and the Worldwide Fund for Nature Pakistan. Together, these organizations teach communities ways to conserve the area.

As part of the project, a hunting ban has been put in effect, and **poaching** has been reduced. People are learning how to plant seedlings to replace trees that have been cut down. Wildlife viewing tours earn money for local communities.

The World Wildlife Fund (WWF) works with groups like the MACP to help protect animals and the environment.

Legends of K2

For many years, legend has stated that K2 carries a curse on women. The curse is said to have started with the first woman to reach the K2 summit, Poland's Wanda Rutkiewicz. Although Rutkiewicz stood atop the mountain's peak in 1986, she died climbing another mountain six years later. France's Chantal Mauduit also reached the summit, but like Rutkiewicz, died climbing another mountain. Three other women reached the summit but died during their descent.

In 2004, Spain's Edurne Pasaban successfully climbed K2, and she survived the descent. Some people believed that this was a sign that the curse was finally broken. In 2006, two other women reached the top of the massive mountain. Nives Meroi of Italy and Japan's Yuka Komatsu were the seventh and eighth women to climb K2. Both survived the descent.

▬ **Edurne Pasaban's goal is to climb all of the world's mountains that are taller than 26,247 feet (8,000 m). There are 14 mountains in this group.**

Ready to Climb

Climbing a mountain like K2 takes a great deal of preparation. Only the best climbers in the world try to summit K2. However, there are many other mountains that are suited to beginning climbers. These tips can help you prepare for a mountain climb.

Use the right equipment.

It is important to have proper climbing gear. A helmet is one of the most important pieces of equipment. It will protect a climber's head from falling rocks. Climbers should wear boots that have good support. The boots should have a rubber sole that will grip rock and keep the climber from slipping. For overnight trips, a tent, stove, and sleeping bag are needed. It is also a good idea to carry a first-aid kit for minor injuries. An ice axe can be used to grip icy ground.

It takes at least two to make a team.

It is important for climbers to travel in groups of two or more. When scaling a mountain, climbers are joined together by a rope. As the first climber heads up the mountain, he or she places anchors in the ground. The climber hooks the rope into the anchors. Once a few anchors are in place, the second climber starts up the mountain to meet with the first climber. If one of the climbers falls, the rope will catch at the anchors.

Start small.

Before heading to a mountain, test your skill on rock-climbing walls. Climbing walls are made from wood, brick, or plastic and have rocklike features on their surface. Climbers can use these walls to practice. Then, they can try a few small mountains.

Check the weather.

It is a good idea to check the weather before heading out on a climb. Snow or rain can put a stop to the climb before it has started. In cold climates, climbers should wear layered clothing. The top layer may include a parka, or heavy coat, along with thermal gloves, a wool hat and scarf, and snow pants.

Natural Attractions

While some people choose to climb K2, many people visit the area around the mountain. People can take scenic tours of the Karakorams, including K2. Some of these tours drive by the mountains. Others take people on a hike up to one of the base camps. The K2 base camp trek is said to be one of the world's top five mountain walks.

The Baltoro Glacier is one of the standout features of the Karakoram Range. This huge sheet of ice stretches for 41 miles (66 km). Clustered around the glacier are several 26,247-feet (8,000-meter) peaks, including K2. The best way to get to the Baltoro Glacier is by guided tour. Tour companies have many options. People can hike and sleep in tents, or they can take jeeps and stay in hotels in neighboring cities.

Skardu, a city in the Northern Areas of Pakistan, has many hotels and hundreds of shops for tourists who visit the area on their way to the Karakorams. Located at 8,200 feet (2,500 m), it is the starting point for most K2 climbers. Climbers access the mountain using the Askole and Hushe Valleys. From here, they can also reach three other Karakoram mountains over 26,247-feet (8,000 m) and the Trango Towers, a group of granite rocky peaks.

■ **Some Skardu residents have set up shops that sell goods for tourists and climbers.**

Pakistani Recipe

Tourists may try Pakistani foods while on their way to K2. Rice is a staple food in Pakistan. For a special treat, it is cooked as a desert called kheer. With an adult, try making this rich rice pudding.

You will need:

1/2 cup basmati rice
4 cups milk
1/4 cup raisins
1 cup sugar
1 tsp cardamom (or nutmeg)
1/4 cup shredded almonds
1/2 cup water

What to do:

1. Soak the rice in the water for one-half hour. Drain the water.

2. With an adult's help, boil the milk.

3. Add the rice to the milk, and simmer on low heat until the mixture is creamy. Stir often so the rice does not stick to the pot.

4. Add sugar, and mix well.

5. Remove from heat. Add the remaining ingredients.

6. Serve hot or cold.

The Effects of Tourism

Pakistan is home to some of the highest mountains in the world. This makes it an exciting place for people to visit. As more people visit the mountains, there are greater effects on the environment and local communities.

Communities that were once very poor now earn money by selling goods and services to tourists. Access roads, airports, and health care services have been built for tourists and also benefit local people.

However, the environment is suffering from the growing number of people in the area. Land has been cleared to make room for hotels and shops. As a result, many plants that local people used as a food source no longer grow in the area. Juniper forests that once grew in the Askole and Hushe Valleys have been used by porters and guides as firewood.

To keep plants, land, and animals safe, locals are learning how to earn money other ways. They are taking part in conservation programs that will help keep the area safe for future generations to enjoy.

Trucks carry products from China to Pakistan via roadways through the Karakorams.

Ecotourism is one way of conserving natural areas. Tourists who take these trips are urged to stay on special trails to keep from trampling the land. In addition, tourists must clear the land of litter by packing all of their trash and other items out of the mountains. Instead of using plants and trees to fuel fires, many people now use a type of oil called kerosene. This helps save trees.

Should people be allowed to tour the Karakorams?

YES	NO
Tourism brings a large sum of money to local people each year. Communities have access to special services as a result.	Tourists harm the natural landscape by littering and collecting plants.
The natural beauty of the area should be shared with any person who can afford to travel to these mountains.	Roads and structures built for tourism have destroyed plant life and animal habitats.
Jobs, such as porters and guides, are created.	Locals rely heavily on tourism for their income. Should fewer tourists visit the area, locals will need to find other ways to survive.

Timeline

Thomas Mongomerie gave each summit in the Karakorams a number. K2 was second in his listing. In 1858, K2 was found to be the second-highest mountain on Earth. It was coincidence, but the name was perfect.

4-5 billion years ago
Earth forms.

40 million years ago
The Karakoram Mountain Range starts to form in Southeast Asia.

1 million years ago
Ice ages begin to occur, shaping Earth's mountains.

12,000 years ago
Erosion starts to shape the mountains of the Karakoram Range.

1856
K2 is surveyed from Kashmir by Thomas Mongomerie.

1858
K2 is confirmed as the second-tallest mountain on Earth.

1861
Henry Haversham Godwin-Austen surveys K2 from within the Karakoram range.

1902
Oscar Eckenstein and Aleister Crowley make the first attempt to climb K2.

1909
Luigi Amedeo makes an unsuccessful attempt to climb K2.

Karakoram Mountain Range.

Red pandas live above K2's tree line.

The people of Skardu use traditional weaving methods.

woman to summit K2.

1987
K2 is measured and said to be higher than Mount Everest.

1987
Mount Everest is measured again and found to be the highest mountain in the world.

2004
Pakistan declares 2004 "The Year of the K2" to honor the 50th anniversary of the first successful summit.

1954
Lino Lacedelli and Achille Compagnoni are the first people to successfully climb K2.

1977
Ichoro Yoshizawa and Ashraf Amman make the second successful climb.

True or False?

Decide whether the following statements are true or false. If the statement is false, make it true.

1. K2 and Mount Godwin-Austen are the same mountain.

2. The Siberian ibex is a type of horse.

3. Thomas Mongomerie was the first person to see K2 up close.

4. Rainfall supplies the lower levels of K2 with all the water it needs.

5. The first five women to summit K2 died.

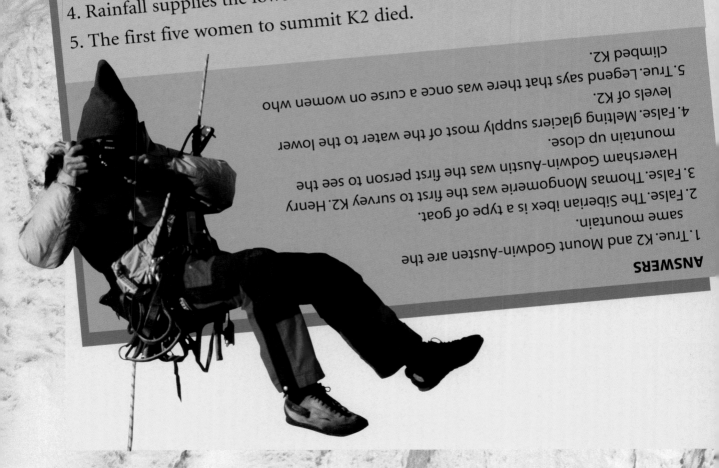

ANSWERS

1. True. K2 and Mount Godwin-Austen are the same mountain.

2. False. The Siberian ibex is a type of goat.

3. False. Thomas Mongomerie was the first to survey K2. Henry Haversham Godwin-Austin was the first person to see the mountain up close.

4. False. Melting glaciers supply most of the water to the lower levels of K2.

5. True. Legend says that there was once a curse on women who climbed K2.

Short Answer

Answer the following questions using information from the book.

1. What is the name of a traditional Pakistani food?
2. What does K2 stand for?
3. Name three types of animals that live on K2.
4. Where do many tourists stay on their visit to the Karakorams?
5. Name the process that forms a mountain.

Multiple Choice

Choose the best answer for the following questions.

1. K2 is part of which mountain range?
   a) The Himalayas
   b) The Rockies
   c) The Karakorams
   d) The Andes

2. To date, how many people have successfully climbed K2?
   a) none
   b) more than 500
   c) fewer than 300
   d) fewer than 25

3. Name the first successful climbers of K2.
   a) Ichiro Yoshizawa and Ashraf Amman
   b) Lino Lacedelli and Achille Compagnoni
   c) Aleister Crowley and Oscar Eckenstein
   d) Henry Haversham Godwin-Austen and Thomas Mongomerie

4. How high is K2?
   a) 8,161 meters
   b) 8,611 meters
   c) 6,811 meters
   d) 1,861 meters

Find Out for Yourself

Books

Gaff, Jackie. *I Wonder Why Mountains Have Snow On top: And Other Questions About Mountains.* Kingfisher: 2004.

Tomljanovic, Tatiana. *Rock Climbing.* New York: Weigl Publishers Inc., 2001.

Websites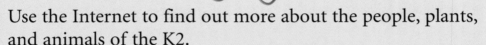

Use the Internet to find out more about the people, plants, and animals of the K2.

Karakorams.com
www.karakorams.com
This site provides information on traveling through the Karakoram Range.

Mountain Areas Conservancy Project
www.macp-pk.org/index.htm
Learn more about the MACP and its programs on this site.

K2—The Savage Mountain
www.jerberyd.com/climbing/stories/k2
This site provides the history of climbing K2.

Skill Matching Page

What did you learn? Look at the questions in the "Skills" column. Compare them to the page number of the answers in the "Page" column. Refresh your memory by reading the "Answer" column below.

SKILLS	ANSWER	PAGE
What facts did I learn from this book?	I learned that the K2 is the second highest mountain on earth. Although remote, people, animals, and plant life survive on the mountain.	4, 10, 12, 13, 18
What skills did I learn?	I learned how to read a map.	5, 7, 16–17
What activities did I do?	I answered the questions in the quizzes.	7, 28–29
How can I find out more?	I can read the books and visit the websites in the Find Out For Yourself section.	30
How can I get involved?	I can be an ecotourist.	25

Glossary

altitude: the measurement above sea level of different locations on Earth

coniferous: trees that have cones and evergreen leaves

conservancy: a group that works to protect an important place or thing from harm

crust: the solid, outer shell of Earth

deciduous: trees that shed their leaves

ecosystems: a community of organisms and the environment in which they live

elevation: the height of something above sea level

erosion: the wearing away of rock by forces of nature

glaciers: slow-moving sheets of ice

ice ages: times during which Earth was covered with ice

metamorphic: rocks that have changed shape due to extreme heat or pressure

monsoons: strong winds in India and Southeast Asia that take place between April and October

poaching: hunting animals illegally

sediment: material that has been deposited by water, ice, or wind

topography: the study of the surface features of an area

Index